Who Was Roald Dahl?

Who Was
Roald Dahl?

by True Kelley
illustrated by Stephen Marchesi

Grosset & Dunlap
An Imprint of Penguin Random House

For the Pillsbury Free Library in Warner, NH—TK

GROSSET & DUNLAP
Penguin Young Readers Group
An Imprint of Penguin Random House

Text copyright © 2012 by True Kelley. Illustrations copyright © 2012 by Stephen Marchesi. Cover illustration copyright © 2012 by Penguin Random House LLC. All rights reserved. Published by Grosset & Dunlap, an imprint of Penguin Random House LLC, 345 Hudson Street, New York, New York 10014. Who HQ™ and all related logos are trademarks owned by Penguin Random House LLC. GROSSET & DUNLAP is a trademark of Penguin Random House LLC. Printed in the USA.

Library of Congress Control Number: 2012014971

ISBN 978-0-448-46146-5   15 14 13 12 11

Contents

Who Was
Roald Dahl?

In 1940, during World War II, Roald Dahl
was a fighter pilot in the British Royal Air Force.
He had to fly a biplane to a secret airstrip in
Africa accompanied by a pilot in a second plane.
Roald was nervous about finding the airstrip. It

was hidden and could be hard to spot. It was also very near enemy lines.

When they took off, it was already getting dark. Roald figured the airstrip was about fifty minutes away. But after about an hour, there was still no airstrip in sight . . . just empty desert, rocks, and boulders. Roald circled the area desperately. Had he been given the wrong directions? He was low on gas. It was growing darker. He had to do an emergency landing. He had to take a chance.

The plane crashed!

Roald's nose was smashed, his skull was fractured, and he was knocked out. The plane

burst into flames. The pilot in the second plane managed to land safely and rescue Roald.

It took a long time for Roald to get better. Did he go back home? No! He still wanted to be a fighter pilot. By the time Word War II ended in 1945, he had shot down five enemy planes. His war adventures in far-off Africa made good stories. Roald started writing about them for magazines.

Today, however, Roald Dahl is not world famous for being a war hero or a magazine writer. Millions of people know him because of the amazing books he wrote for children. In a tiny hut near his house in the English countryside, he wrote such classics as *Charlie and the Chocolate Factory, James and the Giant Peach, Matilda, The BFG,* and *Fantastic Mr. Fox.*

Roald Dahl was imaginative and funny. He invented words like *buzzwangle, zippfizzing,* and *frobscottle* and creatures like Oompa-Loompas and snozzwangers. He remembered what it was like to

be a child, and he knew what children would like
to read.

Roald Dahl is remembered as one of the
greatest storytellers of our time.

Chapter 1
Young Roald

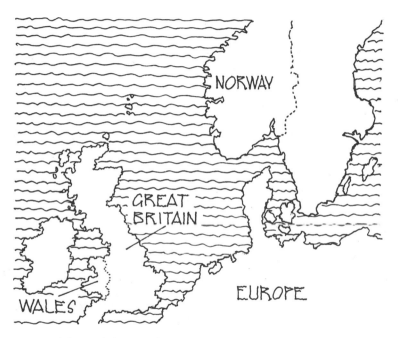

Roald Dahl was born September 13, 1916, in
Wales. Wales borders England and is part of Great
Britain. His parents, Sofie and Harald, were from
Norway. They named him Roald after a famous

Norwegian explorer, Roald Amundsen, who reached the South Pole in 1911.

Harald's job was to provide ships in Wales with coal and supplies. He got quite rich doing it. As a young man, Harald had lost his arm in an accident. Much later, Roald thought it was amazing that his father could tie his shoes faster using only one hand than Roald could with two.

Sofie was Harald's second wife. (His first wife died very young.) Sofie was smart and well educated. Like Harald, she loved beautiful things.

She and Harald had three daughters, Astri, Alfhild, and Else, and one son, Roald. Being the only boy, Roald's sisters called him "the apple." That was short for "the apple of his mother's eye," which meant that Roald was her favorite.

His mother was a great storyteller. She told the children stories about Norwegian monsters, trolls, and fairies. Roald certainly inherited a lot from her!

When Roald was two, his family moved to a mansion in a small village in Wales. They spoke English, but also spoke Norwegian at home. The Dahls were a close, happy family.

When Roald was only about three years old, his life was shattered. His seven-year-old sister, Astri, died of appendicitis. A few months later, his brokenhearted father also died. Sofie was left to care for her three children. She was also raising two stepchildren from Harald's first marriage. And on top of that, she was expecting another child. She had to manage the big house, grounds, servants, farmers, and gardeners. Roald's mother was practical and brave. After baby Asta was born, she moved the family to a smaller house in town. Roald later said his mother was "a rock, a real rock, always on your side whatever you'd done."

Chapter 2
School Days

When Roald was six years old, he started kindergarten. During his school years he sometimes did things that put his mother to the test!

He and his sister rode their tricycles to school, racing down a steep hill and around a corner . . . so fast they were riding on only two wheels!

It sounds dangerous! But at least there was little traffic in those days.

After kindergarten, Roald went to a school for boys. He certainly wasn't the best student. Roald was especially bad at spelling. Even so, he liked to write. He started keeping a secret diary at home when he was eight. He kept it hidden from his four nosy sisters in a tin box high in a tree. Roald would sit way up on a branch and write.

Roald didn't like school. What he did like was stopping by the candy shop with his friends on the

way home. The candy shop was run by a crabby old woman, Mrs. Pratchett. She dug candy out of the jars for the boys with her dirty hands. Yuck!

The boys ate the candy, anyway, of course. But to get back at her, they snuck a dead mouse into one of the jars. The next day, Mrs. Pratchett came

to their school. She pointed out the five boys she suspected. Right in front of Mrs. Pratchett, the teacher took a cane and hit each boy hard on the rear end several times. A cane could leave an ugly welt or scar.

When Roald's mother heard about it, she got really mad. She wasn't mad about the boys' prank. She was mad about the caning—so mad that she sent Roald to a different school the next year.

It was a boarding school for boys called St.
Peter's Preparatory School. Roald was only nine,
and he was terribly homesick. The head of the
school was mean. The boys were caned for

breaking any rules. At
night, Roald slept facing
toward home and quietly
cried himself to sleep.
He wrote his mother
every week. It became a
habit he continued until
she died about forty
years later.

Roald wanted to go home so badly, he faked having appendicitis. This was what his sister had died of. He was sent home, but the doctor there knew Roald was pretending. Back he went to school!

At Christmas, there was a happy surprise at home. His family had a new motorcar! No one knew how to drive it. But his twenty-one-year-old half sister bravely took the whole family out for a

ride. They crashed! Roald's nose was almost knocked off and hung on only by a thread! But fortunately, the doctor was able to stitch it back on.

Every summer, the Dahls went to an island in Norway for vacation. In those days, it was hard to get there. The whole group, ten altogether, had to take taxis, trains, boats, and ferries. It took four days. But what a wonderful place! Their mother

took them on adventures to islands and fishing in a small motorboat. They called it the Hard Black Stinker. Fearless Sofie could handle the boat even in big waves.

In 1927, the Dahl family moved to Bexley, near London. Their new house had a tennis court and gardens. The new neighbors did not think

Mrs. Dahl was a proper parent. She let her kids
run wild and use bad language. They thought that
she was not nearly strict enough!

When Roald was thirteen, he left his family
(and his pet mice, Montague and Marmaduke)

to go to another boarding
school. It was called Repton
School. In many ways,
Repton was even worse than
St. Peter's. There were more

MONTAGUE &
MARMADUKE

rules and more canings. Not only the teachers but also the older boys were allowed to beat the younger boys. It was lonely and frightening for Roald.

At least Roald was good at sports—hockey, soccer, cricket, squash, and swimming. It helped that he was almost six feet six inches tall! In his last year at Repton, he won the school boxing match.

His teachers did not think much of him.
One wrote that he did not like the way Roald
"so persistently wrote words meaning the exact
opposite of what he obviously intended." Certainly
his teacher never expected Roald to become a
great writer.

Was there anything Roald liked about
Repton? Yes! It was near the town where Cadbury

chocolates were made!
The Cadbury Company
often asked students to
rate their chocolate bars.
The boys took these duties
very seriously. Roald
always loved chocolate!

There was the germ of an idea for a great book
there: *Charlie and the Chocolate Factory.*

At Repton, Roald took up photography. He
spent hours in the
darkroom and won
prizes for his photos.
Roald also found
other ways to escape
the terrors of Repton.
Sometimes he took
long walks. Then he

bought a motorcycle and hid it in a garage a few
miles from school. On Sundays he raced about
the countryside, wearing a hat, scarf, and goggles.
He was hoping to disguise himself. If he had been
caught, he would have been kicked out of school.

By July 1933, Roald Dahl was more than ready to leave school. He had had enough! Unlike most of his classmates, though, he did not go on to college. He wanted to see the world.

Chapter 3
Adventures

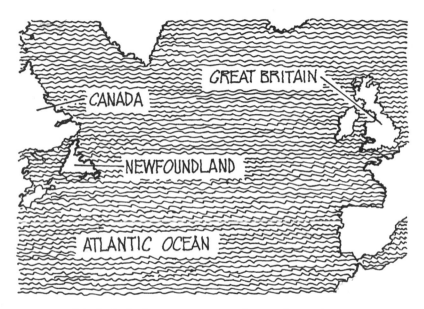

Roald didn't have to wait long for adventure.
He traveled across the Atlantic Ocean to
Newfoundland with a group of about forty
boys. The group was called the Public Schools
Exploring Society. For the last twenty days of the

trip, the twelve strongest boys, including Roald,
carried packs that weighed over one hundred
pounds. Roald needed help just getting his pack
on his back. They slogged through rain, mud, and
swamps. They slept on wet ground in leaky tents.

The mosquitoes were terrible. Roald shaved his head and coated it with tar to keep them from biting! The boys tried to live off the land. But

they couldn't find much to eat except berries and boiled lichen. They were starving and miserable. All they could think and talk about was food.

When this awful trip was over, though, Roald felt strong. He felt like he could handle anything!

Roald got a job in the oil business at Shell Oil Company. He hoped to travel to foreign countries where the company had offices. But Roald was stuck in an office in London. It was dull work. He took the train to work every day, wearing a suit and bowler hat and carrying an umbrella. He looked like a boring middle-aged man.

AN ORIGINAL IDEA

AT AGE 21, WHILE WORKING FOR SHELL, ROALD MADE AN INTERESTING CHOICE: HE HAD MOST OF HIS TEETH PULLED OUT AND REPLACED WITH FALSE TEETH! HE BELIEVED THAT REAL TEETH WERE MORE TROUBLE THAN THEY WERE WORTH WITH ACHES AND DENTAL WORK. HE TALKED HIS MOTHER INTO DOING IT, TOO!

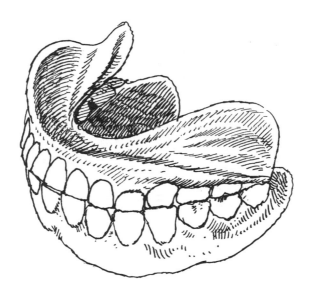

After more than three years, Roald finally had his chance to go abroad. Shell was sending him to Africa!

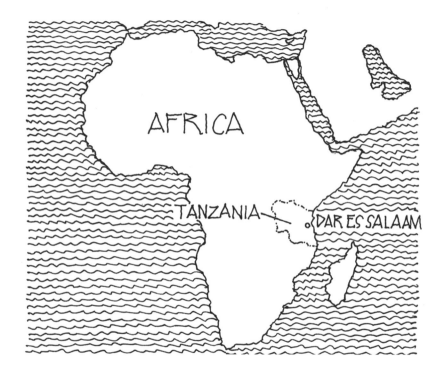

Roald boarded an old ship for the two week voyage to what is now Kenya. Then he got on another smaller boat for two more days. It took him to Dar es Salaam in what is now Tanzania.

He saw palm trees and tropical
splendor for the first time.
This was what he had
hoped for!

He lived in Dar es Salaam
with two other young
Englishmen who also worked
for the company. They had
a house with servants, a
gardener, and a cook. Roald's personal servant,
Mdisho, became a great friend. He taught Roald
to speak Swahili, the language of an African tribe.
Roald, in return, taught him to read and write.

Roald got to see many of the wonders of Africa—animals like hippos, elephants, lions, and giraffes. There were dangers like crocodiles and poisonous snakes. He once killed a deadly black mamba snake with his hockey stick. He said the snake was as thick as his arm and eight feet long.

THE BLACK MAMBA SNAKE

THE BLACK MAMBA OF AFRICA IS THE LONGEST POISONOUS SNAKE, UP TO FOURTEEN FEET. THE BLACK MAMBA IS VERY FAST. IT CAN GO 12.5 MILES PER HOUR! IT'S ACTUALLY NOT BLACK, BUT HAS OLIVE TO GRAY SKIN. IT GETS ITS NAME FROM THE BLACK INSIDE ITS MOUTH, WHICH YOU SEE WHEN IT IS ABOUT TO STRIKE. A BLACK MAMBA IS SHY AND AVOIDS HUMANS, SO ATTACKS ARE RARE. BUT IF CORNERED, IT WILL RISE UP HISSING LIKE A COBRA AND STRIKE REPEATEDLY. WITHOUT ANTIVENIN, YOU'D BE DEAD IN TWENTY MINUTES. IN ROALD'S TIME IN AFRICA, THERE WAS NO ANTIVENIN.

The heat was terrible. Roald got malaria. Later, he turned some of his experiences in Africa into stories. He thought later that living in Africa taught him how to look after himself.

Those skills were about to serve him well. World War II was breaking out. Roald jumped right into the thick of it.

Chapter 4
The Flying Hero

World War II began in Europe in 1939.
Germany invaded Czechoslovakia and then
Poland. In 1940, Germany invaded France and
soon was bombing London. Roald worried about
his family. They lived so close to London. He
begged his mother and sisters to move to a safer
place. His mother was stubborn. They stayed put.

Roald decided to join the British Royal Air
Force (RAF) in Africa. He felt it was the right
thing to do. It also seemed like fun to fly planes.
A pilot friend had taken Roald on a patrol flight.
Roald got very excited about seeing Africa from
the air. He drove nine hundred miles to Nairobi
to begin training with the RAF. The car trip was
an off-road adventure.

THE LONDON BLITZ

BLITZ MEANS LIGHTNING IN GERMAN. ON SEPTEMBER 7, 1940, HITLER SENT THE FIRST OF HUNDREDS OF PLANES TO BOMB LONDON. HE HOPED TO BREAK THE WILL OF THE BRITISH PEOPLE. THE BOMBS FELL FOR TWO HOURS AND THEN A SECOND ATTACK LASTED ALL NIGHT. MUCH OF THE CITY WAS ON FIRE.

THE BOMBS FELL FOR SEVENTY-SIX DAYS AND NIGHTS. AIR RAID SIRENS TRIED TO WARN PEOPLE WHEN AN ATTACK WAS COMING. PEOPLE

TOOK SHELTER IN SUBWAYS OR WHEREVER THEY
COULD. LONDON AND OTHER TOWNS WERE BOMBED
FOR EIGHT MORE MONTHS. MORE THAN A MILLION
BUILDINGS WERE DESTROYED. OVER 43,000
PEOPLE WERE KILLED IN THE ATTACKS. IN ONE
BOMBING IN APRIL, ONE THOUSAND LONDONERS
DIED AND TWO THOUSAND FIRES BURNED. THE
BLITZ ENDED WITH ONE FINAL RAID ON MAY 10,
1941. IT KILLED 1,400 PEOPLE. FIRES BURNED FOR
THREE DAYS. STILL, THE BRITISH PEOPLE BRAVELY
REFUSED TO SURRENDER.

Roald went past herds of giraffes and across raging rivers.

Finally, he got to Nairobi and learned to fly Tiger Moth biplanes. His nickname was "Lofty" because he was so tall (6' 6"). He could barely squeeze into the cockpit. His head stuck up above the windshield!

After less than eight hours of training, he flew solo. He loved it! He could fly low and watch herds of gazelles, flamingos, and giraffes. He learned to loop the loop and fly the plane upside down.

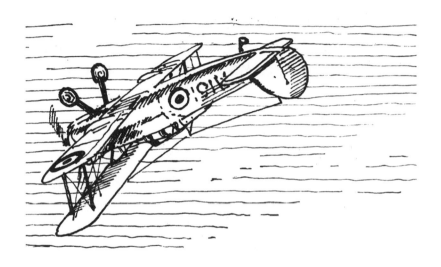

To be a fighter pilot, Roald also had to fly bigger planes armed with machine guns. He trained in the hot desert of Iraq for only six months. Sixteen men were in his training group. Only three lived through the war.

THE ROYAL AIR FORCE

THE ROYAL AIR FORCE WAS FORMED IN 1918. IT IS THE OLDEST AIR FORCE IN THE WORLD. IN 1940, IN WORLD WAR II, THE RAF FOUGHT OFF THE GERMAN AIR ATTACK ON ENGLAND IN THE BATTLE OF BRITAIN. THEY STOPPED HITLER FROM TAKING OVER THE UNITED KINGDOM. THE RAF BOMBED GERMAN CITIES AND USED "BOUNCING" BOMBS TO DESTROY GERMAN DAMS AND CAUSE FLOODS AND POWER LOSS.

Pilot Officer Dahl first had to join his squadron in the desert of North Africa. On his way there, Roald crashed his plane! He barely survived. He had head injuries, and his face was so swollen, he was blind.

Roald was rescued and taken to a hospital. He spent two months in bed. Little by little, his sight came back. But he had terrible headaches. He later came to believe that his brain injury was what turned him into a writer and that it made him more creative.

Roald spent five more months in a hospital in Egypt. For the second time in Roald's life, a doctor rebuilt his nose. This time, he tried to make it look like a movie star's nose! After another month, Roald was patched up and ready to fly again.

He now had to fly a completely new kind of plane. After only two weeks of training, he was ordered to Greece to fight the German Nazis. The flight to Athens took almost five hours. By the time he got there, he was so stiff that he had to be lifted out of the cockpit.

The next weeks were the most dangerous ones in Roald Dahl's life. Roald had no air-to-air

combat training. The Greeks and British were
greatly outnumbered by the enemy. The odds
were terrible.

On his first mission, he shot down a German plane and chased off several others trying to bomb the harbor. He flew twelve missions in four days. Every day he expected to die.

In April 1941, his squadron fought in a long, hard dogfight. It was about two hundred enemy planes against fifteen RAF planes. The British lost three pilots and five planes. They shot down twenty-two enemy planes. Roald Dahl described the Battle of Athens as an "endless blur of enemy fighters whizzing towards me from every side." He fought with skill and bravery. It had been the longest, most intense two weeks of his life. In all his war service, he shot down at least five enemy airplanes. That made him a flying ace.

Roald's headaches came back. Now he was having blackouts, too. It was too dangerous for him to fly. He was sent back to England. As he had feared, the Dahls' home in Bexley had been bombed. But his family was fine. They had moved

to a safer place. He hadn't seen his family in three years. Everyone treated him like a hero . . . and he was! But Roald Dahl would miss flying for the rest of his life.

Chapter 5
America

After the danger of war, Roald rested quietly at home in the country. Even though he didn't have much money, he started collecting art and antiques.

In 1941, the US entered the war to help the Allies (Great Britain, France, and in time Russia). Roald took a job in Washington, DC, at the British Embassy. In his Royal Air Force uniform,

he was every inch a charming and handsome war hero. He went to many fancy Washington parties. He met interesting and glamorous people. Roald became friends with author Ian Fleming, who wrote the James Bond books. He sparred in the boxing ring with Ernest Hemingway. He played poker with Harry Truman who became president in 1945. America and Britain were friends. Even so, Roald kept his ears open for information and secrets he could pass on to the British government.

HARRY S. TRUMAN

Some people said he was a spy.

Although popular, Roald was known for starting nasty arguments. At parties, he seemed to like making people angry. Why did he act this way? Part of the reason may have been pain from his war injuries. In 1945 alone, he had several back surgeries. He had to stay in bed for months. And he kept having terrible headaches.

It was during this time that Roald Dahl began writing for magazines. It happened in a surprising way. A magazine reporter was sent to do an article on Roald's fighter pilot days. Instead, Roald wrote up an account himself and sent it to the reporter.

ROALD'S ART COLLECTION

ROALD DAHL LOVED PAINTINGS BY FRENCH IMPRESSIONISTS. THEY WERE A GROUP OF PAINTERS WHO STARTED PAINTING IN THE LATE 1800S. THEIR PAINTINGS CAPTURED A GLIMPSE OR "IMPRESSION" OF A SCENE.

WHEN ROALD SOLD A STORY, HE WOULD IMMEDIATELY BUY A PAINTING. THEN HE MIGHT HAVE TO SELL THE PAINTING TO GET BY UNTIL HE SOLD ANOTHER STORY. HE SAID THAT PAINTINGS BY MATISSE, ROUAULT, CÉZANNE, RENOIR, DEGAS, AND SISLEY "DECORATED MY WALLS FOR BRIEF PERIODS IN THE FORTIES."

HE COLLECTED AND LOVED ART ALL HIS LIFE.

"Did you know you were a writer?" the reporter asked Roald. Soon Roald's piece appeared in the magazine. It was the first time that Roald Dahl was paid for his writing. He wrote sixteen more stories for the magazine. Later the stories came out as a book, *Over to You*.

Walt Disney heard about this war hero who wrote stories. He invited Roald to Hollywood. They talked about making a movie. It didn't work out. But his script about gremlins in airplanes was turned into a book—his very first children's book. It was called

The Gremlins (A Royal Air Force Story by Flight Lieutenant Roald Dahl). President Roosevelt's wife, Eleanor, read it to her grandchildren. She liked the book so much she invited Roald to the White House.

By the end of the summer in 1945, the war was finally over. Roald had had enough adventure. Even though he had been living in a world of wealth and glamour, he just wanted to go home and be a writer.

England had suffered during the war. Roald was shocked to see the bombed-out buildings, roads, and bridges. There were food and fuel shortages, crime, and unemployment. Even so, Roald was very glad to be back with his family.

Chapter 6
A Struggling Writer

Back home, living with his mother, Roald began work on his first novel. It was for adults. It was very hard for him to write. Roald was in pain the whole time. When it was finished, he couldn't walk and had to have more back surgery. The problems with his back never went away. In fact, by the time he was sixty-five, he had two steel hips and had undergone six back surgeries! His novel was called *Sometime Never*. It was about a world destroyed by nuclear war. So depressing! It was published in 1948.

WRITING ADVICE

ERNEST HEMINGWAY GAVE ROALD SOME ADVICE
ABOUT WRITING. HE SAID, "WHEN IT STARTS GOING
WELL, QUIT." ROALD BELIEVED THAT HEMINGWAY
WAS RIGHT. IT'S EASIER TO BEGIN WRITING AGAIN
THE NEXT DAY IF YOU START AT AN EASY POINT,
RATHER THAN AT A PLACE WHERE YOU FELT STUCK.

ERNEST HEMINGWAY

Writing never came easily to Roald. Working on a long novel had been particularly hard. He decided to try writing short stories. This wasn't easy, either.

It took him months to write a story, sometimes a whole month just to finish the first page! His stories were darkly funny and had surprise endings. Unfortunately, most editors thought the stories were too creepy.

Roald was over thirty and running out of money. He had some money from his father. But he was losing a lot of it gambling. He liked to bet

on greyhound races. He owned quite a few dogs, hired a trainer, and bet on his dogs at the track. More often than not, he lost.

Then slowly, his luck began to change, though not with the greyhounds. *The New Yorker* magazine, famous for publishing short stories, bought one from Roald and paid well. More of his stories appeared in other magazines. Some of them won awards for mystery writing.

Even though his first novel hadn't sold well, Roald still wanted to write another. He began work on *Fifty Thousand Frog Skins*. "Frog skins" is a nickname for dollar bills. He finished it in 1950.

Unfortunately, even Roald's own agent didn't think it was any good. The agent thought no publisher would buy it. After putting in so much work and time, Roald was crushed. He was losing more money racing dogs. He was thirty-four years old and still living with his mother. It was a real low point in his life.

Even so, Roald didn't want to give up writing. British publishers didn't like his work. Maybe American ones would.

ROALD DAHL'S SHORT STORIES

BOTH *KISS KISS* AND *TO SOMEONE LIKE YOU* ARE COLLECTIONS OF ROALD'S STORIES FOR GROWN-UPS. PERHAPS HIS MOST FAMOUS STORY IS "LAMBS TO SLAUGHTER." IN IT, A WOMAN KILLS HER HUSBAND BY HITTING HIM WITH A FROZEN LEG OF LAMB. THEN SHE SERVES THE LAMB TO THE POLICEMEN WHO ARE LOOKING FOR THE MURDER WEAPON.

IN ANOTHER SHORT STORY, "THE SOUND MACHINE," A MAN INVENTS A MACHINE TO HEAR NOISES THAT PLANTS MAKE. WHAT HE HEARS IS PLANTS SCREAMING IN PAIN.

IN THE EARLY 1960S, SEVERAL OF ROALD'S STORIES APPEARED AS EPISODES ON THE POPULAR TV SHOW "ALFRED HITCHCOCK PRESENTS."

ALFRED HITCHCOCK

Chapter 7
Family Man

Back in New York City again, Roald met a young American actress, Patricia Neal. She had been in plays on Broadway and many movies.

(Ronald Reagan, the future president, starred with her in one!) She was seated next to Roald at dinner, but she didn't like him at all. He ignored her and talked  to Leonard Bernstein, a famous music composer and conductor. How rude! But over time, Roald managed to charm Pat, and they fell in love. When Roald was thirty-seven and Patricia was

twenty-seven, they had a small wedding in New York City and moved into an apartment near Central Park.

Roald and Pat were able to buy a house in England near Roald's mother. The couple lived part-time in England and part-time in America.

In 1955, to their great delight, their daughter Olivia was born. Roald became a stay-at-home dad. He took care of the baby when Pat had acting jobs. They had another daughter Tessa in 1957 and a son, Theo, in 1960. Times were good. The couple hired a nanny so Roald had

more time to write. He thought he might write for children. He made up lots of stories that he told his children at bedtime. He said, "Had I not had children, I would not have written books for children . . ."

Roald wanted to write books that were so funny, imaginative, and exciting they would make more children want to read. He wanted to write something new that kids hadn't seen before. How about a story with an earthworm, a spider, and a centipede as its main characters? *James and the Giant Peach* was in the works.

Everything was going so well. Then their three-month-old son, Theo, had a terrible accident. Theo's baby carriage—with Theo in it—was struck by a taxicab! Theo hit his head and was rushed to the hospital. Baby Theo was temporarily

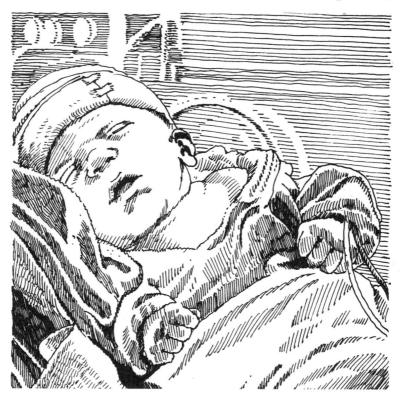

blinded and ran terrible high fevers. In time,
Theo got better. However, he was operated on
nine times before he was three years old. It was
terrifying for the Dahl family. The accident made
Roald and Pat hate New York City. The Dahls
moved back to England.

For a long time, Theo had a drain in his head.
It stopped fluid from building up in his brain. The
trouble was that the drain kept clogging. Roald
was determined to solve the clogging problem.
He worked with a doctor and an engineer and
invented a much better drain. It helped thousands
of children.

ROALD AND WILDLIFE

ROALD ENJOYED LIFE IN THE COUNTRY. HE
GREW ROSES AND VEGETABLES (ESPECIALLY
HUGE ONIONS, HIS FAVORITE!). THE FAMILY HAD
CHICKENS AND A BLACK RABBIT AND TORTOISES
AND BIRDS. THEY HAD A LOT OF BIRDS—OVER ONE
HUNDRED! THEY DIDN'T HAVE ANY CATS, HOWEVER.
ROALD DIDN'T LIKE THEM. BUT ROALD LOVED DOGS!

BESIDES HIS RACING DOGS, HE HAD MANY AS
PETS. HE HAD A BLACK LAB MUTT NAMED JELLY.
HE CLAIMED JELLY WROTE HIS STORIES FOR HIM.
     ROALD'S BEST-KNOWN DOG WAS CHOPPER,
A BROWN-AND-
WHITE JACK
RUSSELL TERRIER.
ROALD SPOILED
HIM TERRIBLY. HE
FED HIM OYSTERS,
CANDY, AND
CAVIAR (ROALD'S
FAVORITE FOOD).
CHOPPER SEEMED
TO UNDERSTAND
EVERYTHING THAT
ROALD SAID. HE
LIVED TO BE SIXTEEN
YEARS OLD. JUST
BEFORE ROALD DIED,
HE WAS WORKING ON
A BOOK INSPIRED BY
CHOPPER.

Roald started working on a new book. It was dedicated to Theo. *Charlie and the Chocolate Factory* was about a boy who is one of five kids to win a tour of an amazing chocolate factory. Roald still loved chocolate!

Once again, when life was going so well, tragedy struck the Dahls. Their oldest daughter, Olivia, died of a rare kind of measles. She was only seven. The family was crushed, especially Roald. His own father had died of grief after losing a daughter at the exact same age. Roald stopped talking and shut himself off from everyone. He couldn't write. Pat, grieving herself, did all she could to hold things together through this awful time.

Little by little, life got better. Roald got back to work on *Charlie and the Chocolate Factory*. He rewrote it four times. In the first version of the book, Roald described the Oompa-Loompas who worked in the chocolate factory as being African

Pygmies. This was changed in later editions of the book. Some people accused Roald of being racist. He really wasn't. Actually, the character of Charlie was originally meant to be black and was based on his old friend Mdisho in Africa.

In 1964, baby Ophelia was born and Patricia won an Academy Award for Best Actress for a movie called *Hud*. It also starred Paul Newman. In that same year, *Charlie and the Chocolate Factory* was published. It was instantly successful. The year 1964 was a happy one for the Dahls!

Chapter 8
More Ups and Downs

Charlie and the Chocolate Factory was a tremendous success. They printed two million copies in China, the most of any book up to that time! Later, around 1970, Roald wrote a screenplay for the movie *Willy Wonka & the Chocolate Factory*.

By 1965, Pat was a big star. Roald's book was doing so well, he was as famous as his wife. The Dahls moved to a fancy Hollywood mansion with a swimming pool.

CHARLIE THE MOVIE

THE DIRECTOR FOR THE MOVIE THOUGHT ROALD'S SCREENPLAY WOULDN'T WORK. ROALD REVISED IT. MEANWHILE, ANOTHER WRITER WAS HIRED TO REDO THE SCRIPT BEHIND HIS BACK. EVEN THE TITLE WAS CHANGED. ROALD REALIZED THE MOVIE WAS OUT OF HIS HANDS. HE DIDN'T LIKE THE WAY GENE WILDER PORTRAYED WILLY, EITHER. (ROALD HAD WANTED PETER SELLERS TO STAR.) THE MOVIE WAS A SUCCESS, ANYWAY, AND BOOK SALES TOOK OFF. BUT ROALD NEVER WROTE ANOTHER SCREENPLAY FOR HIS OWN BOOKS AGAIN. WHAT WOULD ROALD HAVE THOUGHT OF THE MOVIE REMAKE IN 2005, STARRING JOHNNY DEPP?

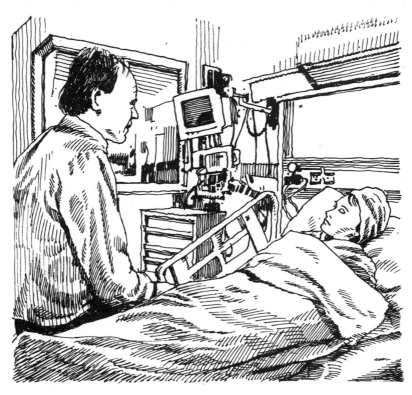

Unbelievably, tragedy struck again. Pat had a sudden stroke. For three weeks, she was in a coma. It looked like she might die! Roald was at her bedside for days. When she woke up, she couldn't move or talk.

After a month in the hospital, Pat went home. But she was depressed. She sat and did nothing.

She could barely talk and jumbled her words. She couldn't read or write.

Roald took charge. He organized neighbors and friends to help get her moving. He hired a speech therapist to work with Pat six hours a day every day. Roald said Pat would be back to acting in a year. The doctors thought he was crazy.

Roald forced Pat to get well. It was as if she was in the army at boot camp. He made her exercise all day. He refused to let her feel sorry for

herself. Some people thought he was cruel. Pat called him Roald the Rotten!

But Pat slowly got better, and she was grateful to Roald! Doctors saw that Roald's tough program worked: They began using the same methods to treat other stroke victims.

The Dahls also had a new baby. Lucy was born five months after Pat's stroke. By the 1970s, Pat was acting again. The Dahls had survived another challenge.

With their new Hollywood lifestyle, the Dahls needed money. Roald didn't like writing screenplays for movies, but it paid well. He wrote a screenplay for *You Only Live Twice*, based on a James Bond book. The movie was a moneymaker.

In 1967, while Roald was in the hospital again for his back, his beloved mother, Sofie, died at age eighty-two. She died on the fifth anniversary of Olivia's death.

Chapter 9
Roald's Hut

"I laugh at exactly the same jokes that children laugh at," Roald once said. He looked at the world in the same way a child does, and he didn't really trust adults. Of course he would be good at making up stories for children!

Roald worked on the script for the movie *Chitty Chitty Bang Bang*. He didn't get along with

the director. Roald was known for being hard to work with. He was touchy, too blunt, and very stubborn about making changes. He lashed out at anyone who didn't like his work. And Roald Dahl's books had many critics.

Some grown-ups hated *Charlie and the Chocolate Factory*. They thought it was tasteless, rude, and too unpleasant for children. Roald was furious that people thought his books would harm children! He said the "shocking ghastly junk" on TV would kill children's imaginations. Still, some of his own stories were shown on TV. Roald was even a host on two shows.

Despite his critics, Roald made a lot of money writing for children. He got fan mail from kids all over the world. Roald said in an interview, "I'm probably more pleased with my children's books than with my adult short stories. Children's books are harder to write. It's tougher to keep a child interested because a child doesn't have the concentration of an adult. The child knows the television is in the next room."

The Dahls now had a home in Great Missenden, England. It was called Gipsy House. Roald did his writing in a small hut in the garden. The hut was a private hideaway where no one really bothered him.

A plastic curtain covered the window of the hut. Drawings, photos, and various souvenirs hung on the walls. The worn linoleum floor was littered with pencil shavings, cigarette ashes, and dust. It was never swept. Roald didn't have a desk. He wrote on a green felt-covered board that rested on his knees. He sat in an old chair of his mother's. The back of the chair had a big hole cut out for the sake of Roald's bad back. Next to his chair was a table with all sorts of odd things on it: a ball of foil candy wrappers, gifts from fans, a geode, and some very old pottery pieces.

ROALD'S HUT

Oddest of all the things Roald kept was a piece of his own hip that had been removed during surgery. And there was a small bottle with tiny bits of spine floating in it! The hut was a quirky place, but Roald was comfortable there.

Roald's day usually began at 9:30 AM. First he went through his fan mail with his secretary. He tried to answer all the letters from kids. Some letters were from sick and injured children. Roald tried to help each of them.  He visited kids in the hospital. He once bought a wheelchair for a little girl.

From 10:30 until lunchtime, he wrote in his hut. After lunch at the house, he might read for a while. Then he'd go back to the hut to write for a couple more hours until supper time. It was said he only slept three or four hours a night.

He was very picky about his writing. He rewrote again and again. For every page he wrote he might throw away three. He said he could never get anything right the first time. It could take him a year to finish a book.

He couldn't type, so he wrote on yellow paper with a certain kind of yellow pencil. He would

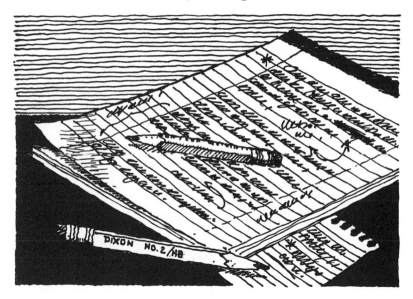

give the messy pages to his secretary, who typed them up. His secretary loved being the first person to read everything!

Roald was rarely happy with any book when he finished it. And right away he would start to worry that he wouldn't be able to come up with a good idea for the next book.

The dedication in *Danny the Champion of the World* is to Roald's "whole family, Pat, Tessa, Theo, Ophelia, Lucy." The book came out in 1975. The dedication makes it sound as if the Dahls were close and happy. But that was not so. Pat and Roald's long marriage was falling apart.

Chapter 10
The Last Chapter

Three years after her stroke, Patricia Neal was working again. She acted in a TV commercial. Pat became good friends with the woman who chose clothes for the actors in the commercial. Her name was Felicity Crosland. Felicity (Liccy, pronounced "Lissy") was divorced. Liccy and her three daughters spent a lot of time with the Dahls. They even went on vacations together. Pat didn't notice that Roald and Liccy were falling in love. They kept it a secret for ten years.

Over time Pat and Roald had grown further and further apart. After being married for thirty years and raising five children, Pat and Roald got a divorce in 1983.

PATRICIA NEAL

IN 1968, PATRICIA NEAL FINALLY RETURNED TO
THE MOVIES IN *THE SUBJECT WAS ROSES*. IT STILL
HAD BEEN HARD FOR HER TO LEARN HER LINES, BUT
SHE WAS NOMINATED FOR AN ACADEMY AWARD!
AS SHE GOT OLDER, PAT WAS OFTEN SEEN IN
PARTS ON TV. THE STORY OF HER ILLNESS AND
RECOVERY WAS MADE INTO A TV MOVIE IN 1981.
PAT GAVE SPEECHES AND INSPIRED PEOPLE WITH
CHALLENGES. SHE WORKED TO HELP CHILDREN AND
ADULTS WITH BRAIN INJURIES. SHE ESTABLISHED
A REHAB CENTER IN HER HOMETOWN OF KNOXVILLE,
TENNESSEE.

PATRICIA DIED OF LUNG CANCER IN 2010 AT
AGE 84.

Roald married Liccy in 1983. He was sixty-seven, and she was forty-five. It was the beginning of the most productive time of Roald's life. It was

also the time when he began his partnership with illustrator Quentin Blake. Liccy said about her husband, "He was not an easy man, but to me he was the most stimulating man in the world and the best husband a woman could ever have."

Roald was a man with many interests. He enjoyed photography, playing sports, raising dogs, and collecting art. He loved antiques and actually owned antique shops with his children. He liked to restore old furniture. He kept vegetable and flower gardens. He grew prizewinning orchids. He collected wine. It was no wonder Liccy found him so fascinating! With all his hobbies, it's amazing that Roald found time to write!

Besides his children's novels, Roald wrote two books about his own life. *Boy* (1984) was about his childhood and school days. *Going Solo* (1986) was about his war adventures. Both books are very entertaining. However, not all the events are completely true. Roald was a storyteller, after all!

QUENTIN BLAKE

QUENTIN BLAKE ILLUSTRATED MANY BOOKS BY ROALD DAHL. HE DID THE ARTWORK IN *THE ENORMOUS CROCODILE, THE TWITS, THE WITCHES, GEORGE'S MARVELOUS MEDICINE, THE GIRAFFE AND THE PELLY AND ME, REVOLTING RHYMES, ESIO TROT,* AND *DIRTY BEASTS,* A BOOK OF POEMS, TO NAME A FEW.

QUENTIN BLAKE'S ILLUSTRATIONS WERE QUIRKY, FUNNY, AND LIVELY. ROALD THOUGHT THEY WERE PERFECT FOR HIS STORIES. ROALD DESCRIBED HIM AS "THE FINEST ILLUSTRATOR OF CHILDREN'S BOOKS IN THE WORLD TODAY."

IN 1982, THEY WORKED ON *THE BFG* ("BIG FRIENDLY GIANT"), WHICH BECAME ONE OF ROALD'S FAVORITE BOOKS. ROALD ACTUALLY CHANGED THE DESCRIPTION OF THE GIANT WHEN HE SAW QUENTIN'S SKETCHES. THE GIANT LOOKED BETTER WEARING SANDALS INSTEAD OF THE HIGH BOOTS THAT ROALD HAD FIRST DESCRIBED. QUENTIN DREW THE GIANT TO LOOK LIKE ROALD.

Matilda was one of Roald's last books. He had a hard time working on it. His health wasn't good. At one point, he started all over and rewrote every word. *Matilda* was an instant best seller when it came out in 1988.

Roald wrote *Esio Trot, The Minpins,* and some adult stories. He wrote a cookbook with Liccy. His brain wasn't slowing down, but his body was. Roald was diagnosed with a rare blood disease.

On November 23, 1990, Roald Dahl died at age seventy-four.

His family buried him near his house with some pencils and wine and chocolates.

Right up to the end, Roald kept working on new ideas. One was about a girl and her dog who understood each other's languages. What a loss not to read that story!

His life was full of wonderful ups and terrible downs. Roald Dahl was an up-and-down person, too. Charming one minute, nasty the next. Self-centered, then generous. His family sometimes found him difficult, but they loved him very much. As Liccy said, "He was a sparky man." What does that mean?

In *Danny the Champion of the World*, Roald had written, "A STODGY parent is no fun at all! What a child wants—and DESERVES— is a parent who is sparky!" So *sparky* means interesting, funny, energetic, and young at heart.

Roald Dahl was a sparky writer as well. His books were exciting and funny, imaginative, and sometimes even scary. He understood what children found interesting.

He would be proud to know that many children all over the world love to read because of his books.

THE ROALD DAHL FOUNDATION

ROALD DAHL WANTED THE MONEY THAT HE MADE TO GO TO GOOD CAUSES. WHILE HE WAS ALIVE, HE WAS GENEROUS TOWARD MANY HOSPITALS, CHARITIES, AND INDIVIDUALS.

AFTER HE DIED, LICCY STARTED THE ROALD DAHL FOUNDATION TO CONTINUE GIVING TO WORTHY CAUSES. IT HAS NOW BECOME ROALD DAHL'S MARVELLOUS CHILDREN'S CHARITY (HTTP://WWW.ROALDDAHLCHARITY.ORG).

BECAUSE SO MANY PEOPLE IN ROALD'S FAMILY SUFFERED BRAIN INJURIES, THE CHARITY GIVES GRANTS IN NEUROLOGY, THE STUDY OF THE BRAIN.

ROALD BELIEVED THAT READING WAS VERY IMPORTANT. HE SUPPORTED CAUSES THAT HELPED KIDS READ AND WRITE. IF YOU GO TO GREAT MISSENDEN, ENGLAND, TODAY, YOU CAN VISIT THE ROALD DAHL MUSEUM AND STORY CENTRE (HTTP://WWW.ROALDDAHLMUSEUM.ORG).

TODAY, TEN PERCENT OF THE AUTHOR ROYALTIES MADE FROM ROALD DAHL'S WORKS GO TO CHARITIES. IN 2010, ONE PUBLISHER SOLD A BOOK BY ROALD DAHL EVERY FIVE SECONDS . . . THAT'S A LOT OF MONEY!

Some of Roald Dahl's Books for Children

How many of these books have you read?

The Gremlins

James and the Giant Peach

Charlie and the Chocolate Factory

Fantastic Mr. Fox

Charlie and the Great Glass Elevator

Danny the Champion of the World

The Twits

George's Marvelous Medicine

The BFG

Dirty Beasts

The Witches

Boy: Tales of Childhood

Going Solo

Matilda

Movies Made from
Roald Dahl's Books

1971   *Willy Wonka & the Chocolate Factory*

1989   *Danny the Champion of the World* (TV)

1990   *Dirty Beasts* (TV)

1990   *Revolting Rhymes*

1990   *The Witches*

1996   *The BFG*

1996   *James and the Giant Peach*

1996   *Matilda*

2005   *Charlie and the Chocolate Factory*

2009   *Fantastic Mr. Fox*

TIMELINE OF ROALD DAHL'S LIFE

1916 —— Born on September 13 in Cardiff, Wales

1929 —— Attends Repton, a boys' boarding school

1939 —— Joins British Royal Air Force in Kenya

1940 —— Crashes plane in desert

1943 —— *The Gremlins*, Dahl's first children's book, published by Disney

1953 —— Marries Patricia Neal

1955 —— Daughter Olivia is born

1957 —— Daughter Tessa is born

1960 —— Son, Theo, is born

1962 —— Olivia dies

1964 —— Daughter Ophelia is born
Charlie and the Chocolate Factory is published

1965 —— Pat suffers stroke
Daughter Lucy is born

1971 —— The movie *Willy Wonka & the Chocolate Factory* comes out

1972 —— Meets Liccy Crosland

1975 —— Begins working with illustrator Quentin Blake

1983 —— Divorces Patricia
Marries Liccy

1988 —— *Matilda* is published

1990 —— Dies on November 23

TIMELINE OF THE WORLD

World War I begins in Europe — **1914**

World War I ends — **1918**

The Charleston becomes a popular dance craze — **1923**

The New York stock market crashes in October — **1929**

World War II begins in Europe — **1939**

The Japanese bomb Pearl Harbor on December 7, and the US enters World War II — **1941**

The US drops atomic bombs on the Japanese cities of Hiroshima and Nagasaki; World War II ends — **1945**

Elvis Presley records his hit "Heartbreak Hotel" — **1956**

Sputnik I is launched into space by the Soviet Union — **1957**

Beatlemania hits the US — **1964**

Martin Luther King Jr. is assassinated in Memphis, TN — **1968**

Apollo 11 lands on the moon — **1969**

President Nixon resigns over the Watergate scandal — **1974**

MTV launches, airing the first music video — **1981**

The Challenger explodes on takeoff — **1986**

The Berlin Wall comes down — **1989**

BIBLIOGRAPHY

Cooling, Wendy, and Quentin Blake. *D Is for Dahl: A Gloriumptious A-Z Guide to the World of Roald Dahl*. New York: Puffin, 2007.

Dahl, Roald. *Boy: Tales of Childhood*. New York: Puffin, 1999.

Dahl, Roald, and Quentin Blake. *Going Solo*. New York: Puffin, 2009.

Houle, Michelle M. *Roald Dahl: Author of Charlie and the Chocolate Factory*. Berkeley Heights, NJ: Enslow, 2006.

Powling, Chris. *Roald Dahl*. Minneapolis: Carolrhoda, 1998.

Roald Dahl's Marvellous Children's Charity. Available at: http://www.roalddahlcharity.org.

The Roald Dahl Museum and Story Centre. Available at: http://www.roalddahlmuseum.org.

Roald Dahl. Available at: http://www.roalddahl.com.

Sturrock, Donald. *Storyteller: The Life of Roald Dahl*. London: HarperPress, 2010.

Discover the Splendiferous World of Roald

Illustrations © Quentin Blake

Dahl

THE WORLD'S No.1 STORYTELLER

Visit **roalddahl.com**
for gloriumptious games and more!

Grosset & Dunlap · Puffin Books
Divisions of Penguin Young Readers Group
penguin.com/youngreaders

Follow that peach!

Join the mission to roll James's giant peach around the world!

Go to
FollowThatPeach.com
for details!

In *James and the Giant Peach*, James and his friends have a fantastic adventure on their giant peach as it travels across the ocean. Now YOU can help James send more peaches all around the world!

www.roalddahl.com
Puffin Books · A division of Penguin Young Readers Group